Supreme Court

Julie Murray

Abdo
MY GOVERNMENT
Kids

abdopublishing.com

Published by Abdo Kids, a division of ABDO, P.O. Box 398166, Minneapolis, Minnesota 55439.
Copyright © 2018 by Abdo Consulting Group, Inc. International copyrights reserved in all countries.
No part of this book may be reproduced in any form without written permission from the publisher.
Abdo Kids Junior™ is a trademark and logo of Abdo Kids.

Printed in the United States of America, North Mankato, Minnesota.

102017

012018

THIS BOOK CONTAINS
RECYCLED MATERIALS

Photo Credits: Alamy, AP Images, Getty Images, iStock, Shutterstock

Production Contributors: Teddy Borth, Jennie Forsberg, Grace Hansen

Design Contributors: Christina Doffing, Candice Keimig, Dorothy Toth

Publisher's Cataloging in Publication Data

Names: Murray, Julie, author.

Title: Supreme Court / by Julie Murray.

Description: Minneapolis, Minnesota : Abdo Kids, 2018. | Series: My government |
    Includes glossary, index and online resource (page 24).

Identifiers: LCCN 2017942865 | ISBN 9781532104008 (lib.bdg.) | ISBN 9781532105128 (ebook) |
    ISBN 9781532105685 (Read-to-me ebook)

Subjects: LCSH: United States--Supreme Court--History--Juvenile literature. | Courts of last resort--
    United States--Juvenile literature. |Judicial process--United States--Juvenile literature.

Classification: DDC 347.73--dc23

LC record available at https://lccn.loc.gov/2017942865

Table of Contents

The Supreme Court

It is the highest court in the US.

It was formed in 1788.

7

It has nine **judges**. One is the chief justice. He is the head judge.

9

The president helps pick them.

11

They hear court **cases**.

They look at the laws.

They decide if a law was broken.

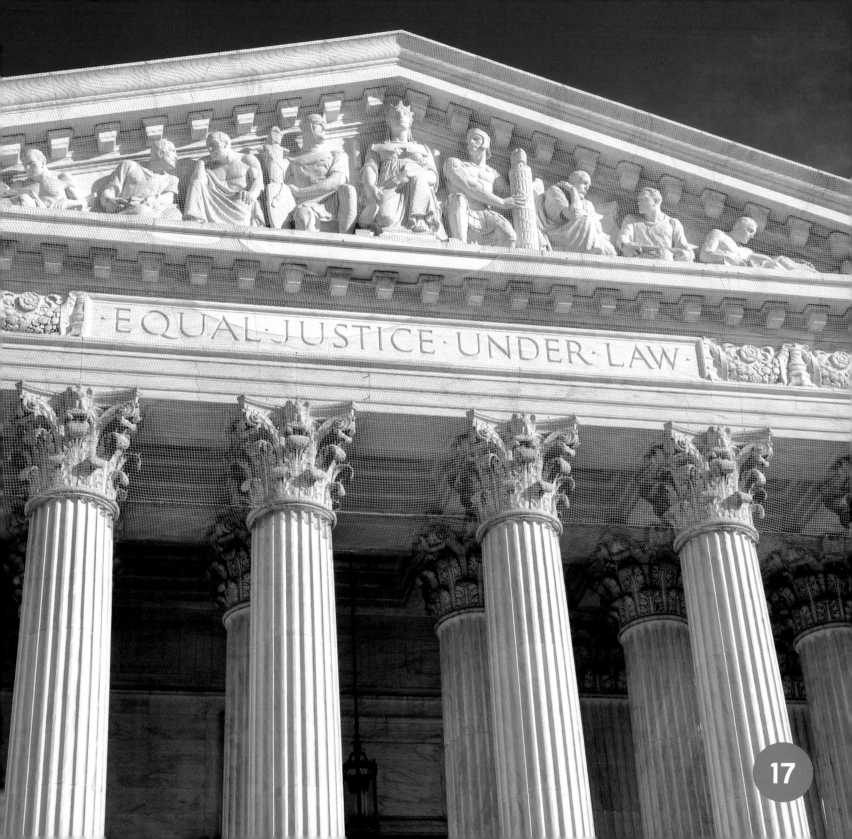

Each **judge** has one vote.

19

Most of them have to agree.

A **ruling** is made. It is **final**!

What is the Supreme Court's Job?

hear important cases

look at laws

decide if laws were broken

make a ruling

Glossary

case
an issue between two people or two groups that is solved by a court.

final
not to be changed.

judge
a person trained to hear and decide cases brought before a court of law.

ruling
a final decision by a court of law.

Index

Abdo Kids ONLINE

FREE! ONLINE MULTIMEDIA RESOURCES

Visit **abdokids.com** and use this code to access crafts, games, videos, and more!

Abdo Kids Code:
MSK4008